QUENTIN TRE'VON HARRIS

# The Dream I Chose to Chase

WWW.13THANDJOAN.COM

*The Dream I Chose to Chase*. Quentin Harris.



13th & Joan books may be purchased for educational, business or sales promotional use. For information, please email the Sales Department at sales@13thandjoan.com.

Printed in the U.S. A.
First Printing, June 2018
Library of Congress Cataloging-in-Publication Data has been applied for.

ISBN: 978-1-7324712-4-5

# *Dedication*

Dedicated to my parents Glenn and Selina Harris, my siblings, Anterrio, Cassandra, Calvin and Salida, and to my son, Aiden Tre'Veon Harris. Thank you guys for your continued support, and I'm proud of you all. I love you!

-Q

# *Epigraph*

"Dream big, work hard."

-Quentin Harris-

# Preface

*My journey from small-town Raeford, North* Carolina to working with some of the biggest names in entertainment inspired me to write this book you're holding, and doing so has been an incredible experience. Within these pages, I discuss my ups and downs, victories and failures, how I survived evictions and having my car repossessed, from working in corporate to being homeless. This book reveals my journey from booking some of the biggest film and radio projects in my life to not going up on a stage production I was featured on the night of the production. Success takes hard work, research, knowledge, wisdom, commitment, dedication, transparency, discipline, and having faith in Jesus Christ.

The purpose of my writing this book is to share ways in which I have been able to turn my dreams into reality. I also want to share with you lessons I have learned along the way that some may see as failures. I have learned to embrace these moments throughout my life and in my career opportunities for growth. Failures often come when our resources don't match our dreams and aspirations. When chasing your dreams, one thing I had to learn was how to fail well. Successful people get knocked down like everyone else, but they take less time getting back up and back out there. In the process of being successful, one thing you'll learn is that you are your only and biggest competition. In this book, I will talk to you about staying the course, completing tasks, holding yourself accountable, being discipline, branding yourself, and much more so that you can enjoy your process without the stress of over-promising or under-delivering. While chasing your dreams, you should enjoy the process. Every day will not be easy, and yes, there will be times when you would like to give up and throw in the towel. However, by the time you're finished with this book, you're going to be ready to turn those dreams into a reality!

# Introduction

I would first like to thank you for reading this book and allowing me to deposit some nuggets of wisdom into your life. Your picking up this book is the first step towards realizing your dreams.

This book is for those who have passion and determination, and for those who may feel stagnant in their career or position. I've also written this book for those who don't have a clue as to where to start. By the time you finish reading my book, trust me, you'll be on the right path.

I've been a part of the entertainment industry for my entire life. I've been performing since I began walking and talking. I was the kid at the Easter Sunday Program screaming “HAPPY EASTER," at church. I have such fond memories of singing in the choir as a young boy. Not only did I want to sing, I also wanted people to enjoy my singing. I absolutely adored the pats on the back and being told how well I did. There were some key people who spoke words that were unforgettable in my mind. A one-on-one with the Choir Director, Mrs. Teresa Torrence, would prove to be one of them. She looked deeply into my eyes and told me that she believed that I had what it took to be successful. "Just burst out of that box and shine like the star you are," she said. I held on to those words and allowed them to carry me towards my purpose.

I want the same for you. It is my hope that in reading this book, you will find purpose, passion, ideas, and goals that you can put into action. It's time for the world to receive you. It's time for the office door to have your name on it. It's time for the television to have your face on it. It's time for the degree to have your title on it.

Each chapter of The Dream I Chose to Chase will help you to be more effective in coming into your own in building relationships, establishing trust, and mastering the art of persuasion. This book is divided into ten steps to assist you in turning your dreams into a reality. You'll learn critical tools, such as embracing who you are and sharing yourself with the world.

It is my goal to help you to identify your motivations and what drives you. We will discuss looking the part which includes working out, eating right, and getting plenty of rest, as well as grabbing the attention of your targeted audience. The time is now to turn failures into victories, and to enjoy the fruits of success while turning those dreams into a reality!

# *Table of Contents*

# Step 1.

## Dreams Are Real

*Hey Dreamer! I'd like to formally introduce myself.* My name is Quentin T. Harris, and I am from Raeford, North Carolina. Like you, I too am a dreamer. I congratulate you for chasing your dream. If no one has told you thus far, allow me to be the first to say that I believe in you! One of the greatest gifts we have been given in life is the ability to dream. Every success begins with a dream.

Before we move further, we must find out what exactly it is you've always wanted to do. Maybe you didn't have the resources, connections, funds, or motivation, or you didn't know where to start. Now is the time! Let's write your dreams down:

1.

2.

3.

4.

5.

Once we figure out what it is you've always wanted to do, then we can begin to find your purpose and your passion. Knowing your purpose for being on this earth is so important. I've seen so many people miss their season of success because they weren't operating with their purpose in mind. The majority of the time when we aren't operating within our purpose it is because we are focused on what others are doing and how ahead of us they are. It is also possible that when we don't have a clue as to what our purpose on earth is, we waste valuable time.

We've all been given a duty here on earth, and it's up to us to figure it out. Once we align ourselves with our purpose, greatness can come in and flood our lives with the blessings God has for us. Some of us have been called to serve. Some have been drawn into politics. Some have been called into the arts or the world of entertainment. For others, corporate america has been the path of choice. No matter what direction you've decided to travel, my purpose is to make sure you are maneuvering towards excellence.

Take your desires and goals and use them in a way that inspires, changes, and elevates others. Your passion and dreams should fuel you to want to be great. Purpose is that thing that you can't stop thinking about, and you can't get enough of it. You wake up doing it, or you go to bed thinking about it. Yep! That's it! That activity, dream or aspiration that just crossed your mind is the very one that

I want to speak life into. I desire to decree and declare prosperity over that one thing in your life. It's that thing I'm willing to help you manage by reading this book. Once you know your purpose, everything else is about strategy, passion, dreams, and reality. Your dreams have to be bigger than your fear.

When accomplishing your dreams, you must set deadlines for yourself. The deadline is your desired completion day, so consider your deadlines as goals. You have to be in the mindset that you are willing to do whatever it takes to see those dreams turn into realities. As dreamers, there are many things in which we can discover success. The more goals we have, the more challenging the journey. Every idea has to reach its point of manifestation.

However, I'm here to be honest with you. Each dream will not work, and you're going to go through many trial and error stages. Every idea will not work. I don't care how many degrees you have, or how well you can sing, or how long you've been in your field. The objective must be to set realistic goals and deadlines to help you become successful. If you're ready to put the work in, inclusive of late nights and early mornings, and a consistent grind, let's prepare for the next level, shall we? Knowing our purpose on earth primes us to turn every idea and dream into a tangible goal. Okay, let's get to it!

# *Step 2.*

## *Embrace Your Life...and Learn*

*If you spend all of your time thinking about people* who aren't thinking about you, how will your dreams come true? Since we are both dreamers, I'm here to share my experiences with you. I'm going to be honest and keep it genuine. This journey towards success can be extremely discouraging, but success is a formula. It is an equation that takes people a lifetime to solve, and in most cases, they go the race never finding the answers. In this book, I'll be teaching you how to unfold the formula, even as I'm still learning it myself. Success begins by choosing the right circle of friends, having mentors, looking the part you're working hard to become, and being knowledgeable in your field. In Learning to embrace your life, you must first be honest with yourself. Are you eating right? Are you studying your craft? Are you feeding your brain and spirit with positive things? There are simple steps that I use daily to help me keep my focus. You can't operate in greatness cluttered down with a lot of unnecessary weight. I recommend learning some skills about life that will keep you on the right path, and here are just a few that I use:

1. Organize and clean every square inch in the house.

2. Donate or trash unneeded clothes, accessories, shoes, appliances, electronics.

3. Delete all phone contacts that aren't being used.

4. Clean desktop and laptop files.

5. Clean cell phone pictures and videos.

6. Unfollow all people who post negative content on social media.

7. Evaluate circle of friends and then redraw your circle.

Now these things may not mean much to some, but you purchased this book to get my take on things and how I stay motivated and focused. Once these things are done, I am allowed time and space to learn who I am, what I am, and who I'm becoming. You can't become a motivational speaker if all you follow on social media are negative videos with bad content. You must learn that the more positive activities you feed your spirit, the more positive you're willing to become. Embrace your life and begin to love everything about you, from your ethnic background to your shape and size. The more in love you are with you; the more everyone else will love you. Identify your personal strengths and how you can use them in your journey to success. Wait! Let's pause right here. I want you to write down five of your personal strengths:

1

2.

3.

4.

5.

The reason I wanted you to write them down is because they play a major role in the effectiveness of capturing your targeted audience when approaching them about your dreams. It is necessary for others to see that you have embraced who you really are, and your self acceptance will empower them to accept you and enhance your possibilities of unlimited accomplishments. I've learned the hard way that being successful and happy in life will require us to really be ourselves and showcase our true personalities. It's such a simple thing to say, but it is a difficult thing to discover and implement. Take note: the number one mistake you can make is watering down your true self because you're afraid others can't handle the 100-proof version of you. Many people go to great lengths to hide their true selves because they fear who they are is not the person they're supposed to be. Erase all of that because you are supposed to be you. Reach for those stars and don't you dare allow fear and insecurity to over take you.

I had to learn to embrace that I talk a lot; I guess you can see that in my book. I was always and still am so loud. I used to get in so much trouble at school for talking, talking, and talking! That was just one of those things I had to accept about myself. One day I was talking to a producer of a radio station, and we were discussing reality television, which is one of my dirty cravings. I can watch it for hours and will not miss a beat. Anyway, the producer looked at me and said, "Wow, you're passionate about this drama and gossip," so I had to admit I loved it. Accepting me for who I was landed me a small segment on Hot 104.5 in Fayetteville, North Carolina called Celebrity Buzz Feed. I wouldn't have ever been granted that opportunity if I weren't myself. To be true, it was only about a two minute segment, but I prepared and ensured that I was ready! I would have my notes all lined up in front of me; I was ready to bring the juiciest stories, yet remain professional. I'm so happy I never despised small beginnings, because during my move to Atlanta, I was granted another opportunity on WTNT 107.7 by having my own radio show called 'Q In The Streets.' It's all about never despising small beginnings, but embracing who you are, and learning to use your authentic self to work for you.

Before I received my own show, there were several times many major networks told me" no!" I'm sure you've already been told no throughout your journey, but I'm here to tell you and grant you a yes. I am saying "yes" to you. Learn from those no's and become great. Become so great they can't tell you no and strive to help them know who you are before you walk into the room. Even though I was told no through various radio stations, I embraced who I was and continued to reach for the stars. Not only was I allowed on radio, but I was able to have my own show with an amazing co-host; it still baffles me. When you know who you truly are, you are able to listen and talk, build trust, and be with people of all ages, sexes, cultural groups, and income levels. You'll always reach better destinations by being you and learning from mistakes.

# *Step 3.*

## *Study Success*

*There are so many ways we can study success. Look at* the way some of the major Fortune 500 Companies have succeeded. The only thing they did was study success branding strategies which are so important. I learned early to not sell products and services. I learned to not sell features, prices, or fancy bells and whistles. In marketing, the most successful brands sell the why, the benefits, and the feelings.

1. Coke vs Pepsi

2. Apple vs Samsung

3. Google vs Bing

4. Nike vs Everybody

5. McDonald's vs Everybody

Coke loses to Pepsi in its blind taste test every time, but why is Coke a bigger brand? Bing beats Google on the blind search engine test, but when's the last time you "Binged" something? Apple's iPhone doesn't even fall into the top three smartphones, but why is Apple's iPhone still the dominant brand? McDonald's gets the most slander in the world. You're shamed for working there and eating there, yet they are the biggest brand in the fast food industry. Something's up. What is it?

Disney, Gucci, Ralph Lauren, Coke, Nike, Apple, McDonald, BMW and Starbucks are brand empires that APPEAL TO EMOTIONS. They don't focus their marketing on affordable prices and nice features. They focus on marketing the benefits they offer that will appeal to your emotions and five senses of sound, smell, feel, sight, and taste. Those last longer in our minds. It's hard to remember a feature or price you paid for a product over the feeling and the sense it gave you .

Business owners understand your "why", and then help turn visitors of your brand into shoppers, shoppers into customers, customers into members, members into advocates, and advocates into raving fans that are down with the brand. People support you, but you have to put the work into your brand! These major companies have laid the foundation and blueprint for us to win, but it's up to us to intake the knowledge and thrive! I have a friend who has told me since day one, "If something isn't broken, don't try and fix it; learn from the greats, and don't change the formula." Whatever your dream is, find a person whom you would consider a mentor. It could be someone from television or someone you don't know, but use his career as a blueprint to enhance yours! You can view and see what school the person attended, or what degree was received, or how he or she opened an academy, or whatever the choice of field was. Don't change the formula. The reason I say formula is because it's a science to the madness, but it's up to you to create and keep it as simple as possible, especially if someone has given you the tools to be successful. Research individuals who would be considered leaders in that particular field. Again, you may not know them personally, but use their brand and business as a blueprint for the success of your dream.

List five mentors whose successful blueprints you could follow and use. How can you use the blueprint of their success story and why?

1.

2.

3.

4.

5.

Every successful person needs a mentor. It's not an option; it's imperative. When you change your company, God will change your currency. You can't make money hanging around small minded individuals. I understand that this sounds cliché, but it's one of life's most precious gifts. Being in business sometimes means learning those people in whom you can trust. It's hard to trust people, but at the same time, a lack of trusting can either help you or break you. It can help you determine who is really there to build a team or a brand or help build the company. It can also break you because you have people, in the company, who want to help you "build", but you're too "closed off" to allow them to help. People will quit and leave you high and dry when the entire time they could have been helping you. There are times when you have to accept and humble yourself to constructive criticism!

You will be as strong now as you were then. God is giving you a second wind to fulfill every passion, every desire, every dream. The season for fear is over. Now, more than ever, is the time to ignite that passion within you. Have faith enough to at least try! You learn to lead by following. If you are following someone who isn't following someone—RUN!! When you are in leadership, don't be afraid to ask for help. Surround yourself with people who can actually have your back and be opened to change. You won't ALWAYS be right! Being in leadership will often require us to humble ourselves and accept constructive criticism which could successfully allow the launching of a plan. You must use wisdom on this journey and have guidance. Have a confidant in whom you can be opened and honest, and be willing to listen and take constructive criticism. You can never be the smartest person in your circle of friends or in the room. If so, then there is no one from whom you can learn. How can you grow?

Mentors don't have to be famous or someone in the public eye. You can have a leader right in your hometown. It could be a pastor or even a best friend. One of my mentors is one of my best friends in the entire world, Derek Jermaine. When it came down to my dreams, he was always the first person I told and shared my ideals. He would give me a firm yes, or he would tell me to map it out and see how it goes. When I wanted to move to Atlanta, he was the first person with whom I communicated about it. I remember when I wanted to come to Atlanta to attend a workshop with Cynthia Bailey, and I was only eighteen years old. At that time, my car was without air, had bad tires, and had several mechanical issues, but he told me, "Q, you get one life. Go!" That was the smartest and best decision of my life because now Cynthia is a mentor of mine, and they both have given me sound advice throughout my journey in being a mogul in entertainment and just everyday life. No matter what field you're in, there is always a blueprint and someone who has done it before you. You just have to be willing to learn from someone else. Every successful person has a mentor, and in order to find true success, you need a person of wisdom in your life.

# *Step 4.*

## *Surround Yourself with Greatness*

*We've all heard the saying, "Iron sharpens iron".* How true is that statement to you? Are you really surrounded by what true success looks like? Are you really around the people with whom you should be connected , or are you holding on to dead weight? We must get to a place where the people around us are a direct reflection of what and who we want to become. People should know you'll be successful by the top five people you spend ninety per cent of your time with. There will be people whom you inspire, but your entire circle should not be a "yes man team" or people who only look up to you because you will not grow. Keep yourself surrounded by people who want to see you win. If it's the other way around, you've already lost. Eighty percent of success is Access. You must surround yourself with gatekeepers.

What I mean by gatekeepers is the people who hold keys to gates. If you're a person looking to start your own business, you should be surrounding yourself with other successful business owners. Why? They can show you things that did not work for them as well as things that did work. You can now omit some lessons and move forward with others. Having access to people who are already doing what you want to do is such a blessing because you can always go to them for advice and more. People are placed in your life for reasons. We don't need a million people around us, but it is necessary to have three to four positive and solid people who are like minded in our corner to have our backs and keep anchored.Sometimes your circle decreases in size but increases in value. You don't have to have tons of people around you, but make sure the few you have around you are dominating in their field and are producing greatness! Get around people who can pour into you and are not wanting to take, take and take all of the time. I like to use the example of a water pitcher. If you fill a pitcher with water all the way to the top, and you place a million cups on the table, that pitcher has to fill up all of those cups daily. At the end of the night, that pitcher no longer has any water, and if it does, it barely drips drop by drop to fill the remainder of the cups. That's just like our lives. You can be so busy pouring and pouring into others, and by the time you need something or need the energy for something, you've poured everything into everyone else. You've now drained yourself. Stop feeding people who are only looking to take a to go plate. Stop allowing people to use your energy. Stop allowing people to use your ideas. Stop allowing people to use you and take you for granted. Stop it today!

We must get to a place where we are the dumbest person in the room. I know that sounds crazy, but catch this: if you're always the smartest person in the room, you can never grow because you feel like you know it all. When you're the dumbest person in the room, you have the potential to see what you can become. You see a goal of your greatness and how you can become better. When you see better, you want to do and be better. When you tell your dreams to small minded people, don't expect them to get it or even believe in you. As long as you believe in and surround yourself with like minded individuals, your dreams have no choice but to come to pass. We've all heard the saying, "Birds of a feather flock together." I stand firmly beside this saying, because if you hang around musicians, you'll find yourself picking up an instrument. If you are surrounded by politics, you'll begin to hear your vocabulary change to reflect your political views. If you hang around drug dealers to make ends meet, you'll find yourself looking to sell drugs in a time of need.

My godmother, supermodel Cynthia Bailey, changed my entire life. The very first time she ever met me, she asked me how serious I was about being in this entertainment field. I told her how serious I was. She looked at me and said, "You have to look the persona, and you have to know your craft. You have to fight for it." She said, "I want you to work on your skin, get a teeth whitening service, and work out more." Now, many of you would think she was out of line, but because I was so motivated and charged, I needed to hear the truth! One of the last things she ever said was "you will only be as successful as the top five people that you connect yourself with every single day." She continued by telling me to "step out of the familiar box!" That was in April of 2011, and I was moved to step out of my regular circle of dysfunction and connect with someone who was already where I wanted to be. That is what it's going to take in order for you to be motivated. Knowledge is powerful.

Stop being a person who is talking about being motivated and changed. Be a person who stays motivated and an agent of change! Some people are in your life for a reason, and some are only there for a season. You can't take everybody with you and don't feel badly because you can't. Be selective of your friends and the people with whom you converse. If we aren't motivating each other and discussing future business plans, then I can't sit down and have a conversation with you. Knowledge is power! I want the power to stay motivated so that I can change my entire life! Once you change your mind, your life will change! Give yourself permission to be bigger, greater, successful, powerful, and motivated and don't feel sorry for doing so. You must cut off all negativity. Anything and anybody who isn't bringing positivity to your life should be avoided and cut off. Do not be afraid to cut them off and stop telling your dreams to small minded people. Stop telling your dreams to people if you have to double check their motives. Furthermore, stop telling your dreams to snakes. We get so angry when a snake bites us, but we fail to realize that a snake is only going to do what it was created to do, which is bite. Whether that snake is biting our dreams, biting our ideas, or even backbiting, whatever the case may be, it was created to bite. We have to stop surrounding ourselves with people who don't mean us any good. Let's stop patty caking with snakes! Stop laughing with them, stop having drinks with them, and stop doing business with them. When you discover them for who they are, address the snakes and let them know you see them for who they are, and no, we don't do nice nasty shade! You can miss one of the most important seasons of your life by being connected to the wrong group of people; it's that imperative. Yes, they are going to say you're acting brand new or you've changed or that you are being stuck up. Slightly remind those negative, toxic people of the following: "I may be all of those things you call me, but what I will not do is give up my hopes and dreams to please someone who isn't a positive factor in my life." Consider telling them, "I love you, but I love me and my dreams and aspirations what is most important to me." I will not apologize for surrounding myself with people who want to see me accomplish more. Trust me, this success journey will be a lonely one, but it'll be worth it. You must have the willpower to want more for yourself.

# Step 5.

## Finding Your Purpose

*The two most important days in life are the day you* were born and the day you discover the purpose of why you were born! Moving from perishing into the land of promise won't work if you aren't motivated to stay there. We think that motivation comes from somewhere else, but our greatest motivation is inside of us. The only difference between successful and unsuccessful people is that successful people know where their gift is and how to focus on it at all costs. Once I discovered my gift, pursuing it became my sole focus. After you finish focusing on the insignificant stuff and start focusing more on the promise, you will begin to move in the right direction. We have to commit to taking ourselves to the next level of our dreams every day. Most of the world just wants you to get a job and make someone else rich. Many schools and training programs will steer you toward serving a company while forgetting about your dreams. So my declaration to myself is, "I might be in this place right now, paying my dues and mastering my craft, but my dreams are out of this world!"

When being motivated, you must always have that burning fire down on the inside! Trust me, every day you won't feel like you can take on the world. There are going to be times when you feel like the lowest thing on this entire earth, but you must stay true to that burning fire that lies within you. Your dream and vision should keep you moving forward, even when you don't feel like it. Success is not predicated upon your emotions. You must want success so badly that you need it like your next breath. Remaining motivated is key to becoming successful. Keeping yourself inspired is seeing and knowing exactly where it is that you're going. A great way to keep yourself focused is by writing your goals out so that they are tangible, and you can see exactly what it is you want to do. I'm a firm believer in the day you change your mind and your way of thinking is the day you're going to change your entire life. When you want better, it's going to come to you. When you expect better, it's going to come to you. When you work for better, all you will receive is better, but it's all about changing your mindset! You may not have that dream in your hand, but if you work your "tail" off every single day, it will happen! Loyalty has an expiration date, and you can't continue to hang around the same crowd if you're expecting greater. It just won't work! You need to begin to hang with people who are going to get you to the next level. You must stay motivated and not be afraid of the unfamiliar.

# Step 6.

## Take the Leap!

*Some blessings can be right around the block, but* because we never leave the corner, we will never know it. You may not be where you'd like to be or where you think you should be, but let God handle the process. You can't be in the driver's seat where God is supposed to be and trying to give direction from the back seat. Take the leap of faith and trust the process of your life and let God guide you where you're supposed to be. I believe if you see it you can be it. Learn the law of mental transportation. Every successful person has taken the jump and the leap off the cliff of life. Now that we've found your purpose, let's start with walking up to the cliff of life. Now we have to begin to put some motion and action behind your purpose and what you want to do with it. You can't be afraid to move on, do better, and dream bigger. Sometimes God will give us an idea or dream, and we will sit on it for years because we have become comfortable at our current job, or the church in which we serve, or the state in which we live. I'm a firm believer that if your dreams, aspirations, and goals don't scare you, then you're not dreaming big enough. I know we've heard that before, but it's serious, and we must apply it to our life daily. There will never be a right moment to take the leap of faith that involves quitting your nine to five to embark upon entrepreneurship. There will never be a perfect time to take the leap of faith, but it's required to achieve greatness. In order to be successful, you must step out on faith. When God sees you making a step of faith, He will begin to line things up according to the desires of your heart. Trust me, if God gave you the vision, He will not leave you..

One of my favorite scriptures is Psalm 119:105: "By your words, I can see where I'm going." His words throw a beam of light on your dark path. Every time you delay stepping out and taking the leap of faith, you are delaying the prosperous future that God has for you! What I've learned is that your business cannot grow past your level of thinking. In the event that your business outgrows you, it will eventually fold back into your own level of understanding and problem solving. It's only a matter of time.

Before you take the leap of faith, you have to ask yourself, "am I really ready?" You must study top leaders and successful people. Once you've done that and you know your purpose and goals, all you have to do is take the leap of faith and jump out there. I'll give you a quick mini memory on which I took my very first leap of faith. I remember when I was in the gym with my mentor, Derek Jermaine, and I told him I wanted to go to Atlanta for a workshop that Cynthia Bailey was having. At the time, I didn't have much money or even the transportation to get there. He told me to try it, and I did. The next week, I grabbed my best friend Q, who has the same name, and I asked him if we could come to Atlanta for a couple of days? I also asked if we could stay with his mom who lived here at the time. She approved and said "yes". I was still a senior in high school, so I didn't have much money. We ate meat sandwiches all the way down the highway. Mind you, I was driving my very first car that needed tires and had no air conditioner, and I couldn't drive over sixty-five miles per hour. I was shocked when I learned that the registration fee would increase, especially if you planned to attend more than one day, but luckily I had a favor with one of the conductors who allowed me to participate at no cost.

Let's stop right here for a brief moment. I would have never received that type of favor if I would have stayed home and allowed excuses to get in the way. While I was there, over fifty beautiful guys and girls attended the seminar. Near the end of the class, Cynthia Bailey walked up to me and asked me to stay after class. I was nervous as I didn't know what she wanted. I checked my bag to make sure I didn't steal anything by accident. She walked up to me and said, "I really love your positive energy, and you have a great persona about yourself, but this isn't what you wear to a modeling seminar. I want you to change your hair, and I want you to take better care of your facial skin." Most people would have thought she was being shady, but I took those words to heart and did everything she told me to do. She said, "I think you're too short to model, but have you thought about acting on television or being on radio?" She then paused and asked me to join her for an event that night to meet some industry friends. I didn't have any fancy clothes to meet the hype of what she wanted me to look like, but I had gotten that far. To even receive a personal invite from her to a VIP event meant I couldn't say no. So I took all of the money I had to go and get a fancy red blazer, and I went home and switched my hair into an enormous Mohawk. When I arrived, so many people were taking pictures of us, and I was like, wow! If I had stayed home, I would have never received this treatment or even been exposed to this lifestyle.

Greatness or the dreams you want to reach will never come if you continue to make excuses! Growing up in a Christian home, I have always heard, "If only you had faith the size of a mustard seed." I agree: all you need is a bit of faith some determination, and courage. You must put your mind on your dreams so you can achieve them.. It's all about you and taking that first step towards greatness! If God spoke to you concerning your dream, DO IT NOW! God is so strategic concerning your life, and he makes no mistakes. Everything will not be easy! When a hardship is presented, it's a test to see how badly you really want your dreams to become a reality. Don't allow that window of Grace to close, because you never know when the opportunity will come around again. God told Abraham to just start walking, and He (God) will do the rest. If He spoke to you concerning your dreams, job, career move, or spouse, all God needs from you is to start walking!

# Step 7.

## Embrace Failure

B*efore I start this chapter, can I be honest and say* this was one of the toughest lessons I had to learn? The generation today is always so ready for things to happen overnight. We all want to throw our success in a bowl, add water, and stir for thirty seconds. In reality, we have to get in the oven and go through an entire process. We're always trying to rush the process, so when things don't go our way, we get frustrated. Trust me, I went through many lessons in life where I was ready to walk away from my dreams due to things not happening when I wanted them to or when I felt they should be happening. Let me ask you some questions. “When things are tough, are you willing to continue and keep going?” “When things are rough and you see no direction, do you quit and give up?” “Where is the origin of your determination?” Those are questions you must ask yourself during those times. Take this quick note: You will grow through what you go through. It does not matter what circumstances may be presented to you in life, you have the ability to overcome anything and everything. In order to be successful, you are going to go through many trials and tribulations in order to reach true success. In everything, you must learn to embrace the failure.

My grandmother used to say, "If God will bring you to it, he will bring you through it." That means during those hard times you must figure out how badly you want to turn those dreams into a reality. You must learn to embrace failure. Every day of your life will not be sunny and positive, so you must learn and understand how to get through those tough times and push through the dirt. You must keep your eye on the prize and continue to move forward toward the mark. You can't get passed failure unless you confront it. You have to look failure in the face and begin to speak those things as though they were tangible. What is the formula for success? It's quite simple: Double your rate of failure. You are thinking of failure as the enemy of success, but it isn't at all. You can be discouraged by failure, or you can learn from it, so go ahead and make mistakes. Make all the mistakes you can. Remember where you will find success, and don't be afraid to fail! Failure should be our teacher, not our undertaker. Failure is delay, not defeat. It is a temporary detour, not a dead end. Failure is something we can avoid only by saying nothing, doing nothing, and being nothing. The only real mistake is the one from which we learn nothing. What is the point of being alive if you don't try to do something remarkable? Successful and unsuccessful people do not vary greatly in their abilities. They vary in their desires to reach their full potential. Make up your mind and believe that whatever comes your way, no matter how difficult, no matter how unfair, you will do more than simply survive—you will thrive.

# Step 8.

## Don't Stop!

*Whenever you're trying to obtain greatness, you're* going to always run into hardship. It's about overcoming the hardship and working your way through the process. With process, there is always a period of wait. We must learn to operate through the process; anything sustainable must go through a process to make sure it's well developed. When you see entertainers, actors, and athletes come across our television screen to accept an award, you must believe they've gone through the storm and rain to get where they are. For instance, this book you are currently reading is a part of my process. This time last year, I was living a totally opposite life while writing a book, but I'm grateful because it was a part of my process. Here is a quick story of my not giving up and quitting. Last year, I was evicted from my home on May 11th around 11:30 a.m. That morning I had an urge to get up and begin my hunt for an apartment. I was up with a good brother of mine, and we were out all day riding and searching for the next best deal before the eviction was on my credit. As I pulled into my home and saw my stuff thrown into the streets, someone who was VERY close to me was standing outside near my things.

He said to me, "Q, I was just about to contact you. I saw some Mexicans going through your things, and they even took some stuff." He even saw where they placed some of my son's items in back of the apartment. I was so distraught. Why would someone steal my son's items? The same gentleman said to me, "Q, when you're evicted and your stuff is in the streets, it's free range for anybody to get." At the time, I was staying in a very prestigious apartment complex, so I thought that people wouldn't just go around stealing. At the time when he spoke, not for one second did I stop and think that he would have been the one to snatch items from me. The crazy thing about the twist to this story is he is the same guy who had texted me that morning and asked me how I was doing. God had my back, and He wouldn't leave me and all this other stuff. He was someone in whom I confided, trusted, and even shared my goals and dreams with. The lesson God was trying to teach me was on the journey He was taking me, I would learn that the people that I thought were for me were the people I have to watch. The type of lifestyle and wealth that I was going to have in my life meant that I could not afford to not know those in my circle. It's very imperative that we know our surroundings! He stole some very important things from me such as a very important bag that my grandmother had just given me. It was the very last thing she had given me before she passed away. He stole a touch screen computer that my mother had given me, and he stole all types of designer bags, belts, and shoes. He took some of my most valuable things. I was in shock once I found out he was the one who had stolen my things. I found out from a neighbor of mine, a Caucasian gentleman who happened to be an atheist. He came and told me that he saw a black guy with a white beard going in and out of my things, and he was taking them to different places. He described T, a person I considered to be a friend. Minutes later, I approached the man and asked if he had taken my things, and of course his response was that he had not.

Maybe ten minutes later, I stood in the middle of the parking lot, and I decreed that whoever had my stuff wouldn't rest until they returned my missing items to me. Less than ten minutes passed, and I received a message from Mr. King. I still have the messages in my phone that said he had gone through my stuff and had given my things to a friend of his whom he felt he was helping. He thought this man was in need. By this time, I became furious and wanted to physically fight this man. I'm so grateful my friend was there with me and demanded that I not do that because God could take care of him better than I. I honestly didn't want to hear that at the time, but I knew it was what was best for me. He said he would gather all of my items and have them returned to me. He kept bringing my items out piece by piece. Not only was he giving them back, but he couldn't even face me. He left some of my personal items outside under the steps. Every time I would go to retrieve something, something else would be missing and then I would have to go back. We played that game for three or four times that day.

Now let's rewind and then fast forward. When I got home and saw my items setting outside, I immediately went to the leasing office to ask Ms. Lisa, whom I felt was my guardian angel, if she could at least open the door so I could get all of my items from the house. She said I had about five minutes, but I knew that I have would not have enough time. She must have seen my disappointment. She then told me to come for the key before the office closed at 6 p.m. and added that I could get my things and leave the door opened overnight. In that five minutes of her giving me the key, I IMMEDIATELY dashed across the street in moving traffic to go and make a copy of the key for the new lock. I dashed back across the street to give the key back to her. For over a month, I was still living in the home. I would leave early in the morning and come home late at night. Now some of you may look at it as a crime, but I looked at it as God still making a way. Not once did I ever get caught or did anyone ever question me about being in the home. I had paid the light bill for the month of May, so I always had electricity. When the electricity was shut off, I didn't need much of anything. I would always eat before I went there, and I would shower at the gym where I had attended. I may not have had much, and some would have packed up and gone home, but I had to prove to myself that I was strong, and that I was determined about my dreams. I wouldn't let anything or anyone stop me. Many probably would have called me crazy, but I had to fight for my dreams and prove to myself that I wanted it just that bad. They have now changed the locks on the home.

When chasing your dreams, you might not always have the "best experience" but it's what you make of it. It's all about overcoming obstacles and getting past things and enduring the process that you've had to overcome in former times. I remember an incident that happened on August 17, 2016. I was preparing for a particular production, and I had been rehearsing for it. At the time, I had so much on my plate from planning a homeless back to school event for homeless kids to having my radio show on WTNT 107.7. I also had a host of other things going on at the moment; therefore, I had missed a few rehearsals, but I was still at home studying when I could! That morning I reached out to the director to make sure I had the correct location and time for that particular day, but at 12:06 p.m. Atlanta time, he let me go from the production and told me he understood that I had a lot going on at the time. He said that he had refilled my role and character. I responded in a positive way because you NEVER want to burn bridges in this business. I responded and said, "Thank you so much for the opportunity." I remember clearing the dates in my calendar, and I remember praying to God. I reminded Him that he had closed this door, but I knew He had something bigger and better waiting on me. I began to erase the dates once again in my phone. At 12:34 p.m., I received a phone call with the dream job offer of my life. Being that I had just gone through being homeless, not eating, and more, this offer was monumental. I struggled to get to the interview to get the position. I rode almost thirty minutes through Atlanta traffic in the far right hand lane just in case I ran out of gas. If I did, I could just pull off to the side of the road if needed. I even had to wait and sleep in my car in the hot sun for two hours after the interview was over, but it's about having drive and determination and keeping a positive attitude. Keep going and continue to ask yourself, how bad do you really want it? Never put yourself in harmful situations, but sometimes you just grit your teeth and put up a fight! What I've been through may have killed someone else.

If it weren't for my drive, determination, and persistent desire for success and my being able to endure the process, then some of the things that I've been through could have killed me. Last year marked eleven months since I had been in Atlanta, and it was almost time for me to move into another place of living. There might be some truth in the belief that when you are about to enter into another level of success, the devil begins his work. In the process of my moving from one place to another, I was left with less than three weeks to find a place to stay. I knew that my time was limited for picking up and moving my entire apartment. I didn't know where I was moving, nor did I have a place chosen.. During that process, I realized that my very first, nice, luxury vehicle was all mine to keep. I lived by myself in Atlanta, and I did not have any family here. All of my living expenses were on my own shoulders. I was a few payments behind on my car note, and one night while I was asleep, they came and repossessed my car. Wow, was I devastated? I had no idea how I would get around from event to event, or how I would actually make it to work. Because of the place where I was positioned in my life, I had no desire to give up. I had to show God that I was mature and that I was ready for the next level, so I accepted the challenge that God had thrown my way. I took the best route that I thought was good for me and just allowed the car to go back. I asked my dad to bring up an old vehicle from North Carolina so that I could drive it. Almost a week after my dad had brought the car to me and exactly one day before I had to move completely out of my house, I received a phone call from a very good friend of mine. He had locked his keys inside the car at a nightclub. He had always been there for me; therefore, I couldn't fathom not going and helping him. He called, and I went to help him. We got everything squared away, and I was on my way back home when I was pulled over by the police. I'm now thinking that I am being stopped because it's three a.m., and I am in an urban neighborhood. I also thought that he was just pulling me over because I was wearing a hoodie and driving a cadillac at three a.m. Maybe, he just wanted to make sure I was legal and wasn't drinking. Long story short, he came back to the car and said my license was suspended and my tags were invalid. He had to take my driver's license on the spot. In the state of Georgia, you can't have expired tags passed the thirty day mark, and mine had been expired for thirty five days. You guessed it; they impounded my car on the spot. It's three a.m., and I have on shorts and a hoodie. I'm more than five miles from home, and it's pitch black. Did I mention that my cell phone had died in the process of all of this? I began to walk to to the corner store to ask the store manager of an Exxon gas station if I could charge my phone. This was a gas station where I often got gas almost daily, and it was where I shopped on a daily basis. He told me I was unable to use his store to get a quick charge to my phone. He also told me that if I asked him again, he would call the cops on me. Wow!

All of this was happening the night that I was scheduled to be out of my apartment. The next day my landlord popped up to do an inspection, and of course I'm late and don't have all of my items out of the house. He hit me with late fees due to my not being out of the house. Now, you're probably wondering why haven't I gone home to North Carolina to my parents' home where I could be comfortable and live my regular lifestyle. It's because I'm not afraid of adversity, and I know what my future holds. I'm not afraid to go after what it is that I want. I want to be successful, and I profess that I am an overcomer of adversity! Two to three weeks after I had moved into my new apartment in the heart of Atlanta, "BuckHead", I was working a nine to five job that was beginning to be stressful. Before it was time for me to go to work, I began to pray every single day. On the morning of February 23, 2016, I arose ready and charged to pray, and that's exactly what I did. I got up and called on the name of Jesus, and I cried out to Him in a scream saying, "If it's not meant to be, move it out of my way! I said "if you have greater for me, show me what you would have me to do and manifest yourself before me. Move on my behalf. I'm listening to you, God. I hear you, God." I strategically prayed about my job, finances and career. In this season, I had to be very careful on what I prayed about because God was moving on my behalf! That exact same day my boss called me and said, "Quentin, unfortunately we are making a cut. with the company, and we are going to have to let you go. Q, we love you and are sorry it had to come to this." Then he said, "Q, go chase your dreams!"

I was confused, but I remembered the prayer that I had prayed that exact same day. God didn't give me a plan that day, nor did he give me what he wanted me to do. I didn't have to be concerned about that stressful job anymore. Ii was imperative for me to trust God because I knew for a fact that he had a strategic plan for my life. At that point, I had no choice but to place my all in all into him. I knew every day I would do the same. It wouldn't be easy, but I knew it would be worth it. You have to continue to fight behind the scenes. Your time for greatness will come. The moment you want to give up is the exact moment when you need to push harder. Never give up! When fighting for your dreams, people will only see the public success, but they will never see what you really and truly had to go through. Whenever you see a successful person, you only see the public glories. You never see the private sacrifices they had to overcome to reach their full potential, goals, dreams, and aspirations. Keep going even when noone is clapping and rooting for you!.

# Step 9.

## *Create a Plan (Plan It and Execute It)*

*Ask yourself this question, "Is what I'm doing today* preparing me for where I want to be tomorrow?" The "how" is also an important component to becoming successful, but it is not nearly as important as the why you need to be successful. As you embark upon this journey of turning your dreams into a reality, the "how" question will come up many times. There are so many steps that should be taken in order to be successful. One can feel overwhelmed and become nervous which can delay any action on creating a plan. I remember when I sat down with one of my best friends/mentors in the entire world, Derek Jermaine, and I told him I had an idea of putting together a t-shirt line. I'm not a designer, nor am I into fashion that much, but because of the way I was branding myself, we talked about how people recognized me as "the boy who is chasing his dreams" or the #DreamsAreReal guy. It's all about being visual. Whenever you see the hashtag #DreamsAreReal, you automatically think of me. If people can't see you or can't have something tangible in their hand, then you know the saying, "out of sight out of mind."

One goal has to be branding, and it should keep you in the minds of people.

I had the idea of creating the line, and my mentor advised me to get it done. He said, "do it." In a few days I mentioned my ideal at the dinner table at one of our favorite restaurants, and he asked me about the idea. He did not know that I had already had the merchandise printed and had created the clothing line completed with mocked copies. It's not always about getting it right. Sometimes you just have to get it done without waiting and delaying. I planned a release party and had all of my hometown family and friends attend. I raised over twenty two hundred dollars in one day! Now, I'm not saying you shouldn't have your business in order, nor am I saying that it's safe to just do things without planning. I seriously suggest that you get a business plan, trademark your business, and retain an attorney, but you purchased this book to hear my story. If I had the chance to start all over and do it the right way, I probably wouldn't. I have learned more in my ignorance than I could express in one book, and I will not apologize for being a man of action. I was the type of guy to act first then think later. Again, I'm not saying to start the way I started. It was not the smartest move on my part, but I was more concerned with creating action than creating a favorable outcome. When you're focused on the outcome, it will undoubtedly harness your activity, but if you focus on your activity and completing tasks, the outcome will take care of itself. We often times use the excuse, "I don't have enough time." That's a lazy excuse. We have the same amount of time as Oprah, Tyler

Perry, Kevin Hart, Ellen, and even Beyoncé. We must learn the systems of balance because most of us are mismanaging our time. It's sad most of us will put in an extra hour working for someone else, but when it comes to our own dreams and goals, we're too tired. My advice to anybody who still has a nine to five job is to give yourself an hour a day to work on your dreams. There is no logic in being able to work for someone else for seven and eight hours a day while avoiding being able to give yourself one hour a day to become disciplined to be your own boss. Create a plan that alleviates wasted and non productive time but includes a daily agenda that prioritizes time to work on your dreams..

I challenge you to write everything in a daily agenda, and be as specific as possible from sun up to sun down. Studying is ongoing and not optimal. Try to squeeze as many of your dreams into that day by outlining what you can do to begin turning them into realities. Be intentional in the use of your time by including practical opportunities to develop your mind and body for your chosen work. If you're a model, you need to wake up and exercise, and if you're a dentist, you should spend time consulting with and observing a dentist. With strategic planning, you can sleep well, eat well, work your job, exercise, and still be able to chase your dreams. All of these things are a part of my daily calendar. It's a must that we take care of ourselves while chasing our dreams

Outline your daily schedule and how to prioritize your day:

________________________________________

________________________________________

________________________________________

________________________________________

________________________________________

________________________________________

________________________________________

________________________________________

________________________________________

________________________________________

________________________________________

________________________________________

I made it a habit to plan my day the night before, so I can look FORWARD to waking up .

My nine ingredients that successfully help me to master my time every day.

1. Get up early.

2. Clean your surroundings.

3. Eat well.

4. Eliminate all distractions.

5. Start the grind.

6. Take calculated breaks.

7. Track progress.

8. Plan and prioritize the next day.

9. Get quality sleep to refresh for tomorrow.

# *Step 10.*

## *Do the Work!*

*Yes, I know chasing your dreams may seem scary and* like you'll never get there, but all you have to do is take things day by day. The secret to following a dream lies in one's motivation to get started. During the process of chasing your dreams, never chase money. Success is not gained by how much money you have; it's about mindset and mentality. You must show people that your dream belongs to you and make them believe it. Every time they see you, you should be a walking billboard of your dreams. If you want to be a doctor, you should be in medical school. If you want to sell real estate, others should see you dressed for success in business casual wear. If you want to be a dancer, we should routinely see you exercising, strengthening and working out. You have to paint the picture of who you want to become and make others believe it. Branding is so important, and it's a tool that many people overlook. If you're a dentist, I should see you cleaning some teeth on your Instagram. I shouldn't have to scroll through tons of things to see your work. You must put in the work by remaining consistent even on your social media posting, the way you carry yourself, and how you spend your time. Someone is always watching; therefore, it's important for you to always work on painting the picture of what you want people to receive from you.

Branding is important, even down to the places you go. If you're a youth pastor, there is no reason people should see you in the clubs three to four times a month. Honestly, we shouldn't see you in the clubs at any time. Trust me, someone always has a eye on you at all times. What kind of brand can you have if you're always in the club celebrating? What type of work are you putting in? Ask any of my personal friends, and they will tell you that I am known as the "homebody king". They are always inviting me places, but I'm always declining. Why? Because I only party with a purpose because I have a brand to protect, and I'm putting the work in to make sure I'm successful. If I go to a party or a club, I avail myself because I know a big producer will be there or a public relations company will have a representative I might meet. I only party to network and build business relationships. Now some of you will call me lame, or whatever the case may be, and that's totally fine, but I have to put the work in to be successful. I want to shake that producer's or director's hand or provide them with my business card, then I'm gone. When putting in the work, you must not overwhelm yourself by looking at all you want to accomplish at one time because you'll feel defeated and never begin what you were supposed to have done years ago.

Sometimes, your first step might be to relocate to a totally different city that has a market for your dream. If relocating is something you might consider, begin by researching that city to see what jobs are available. Consider your monthly budget and price homes and apartments in different areas of various cities. Your first step may be to become a model, so you would need to eat healthy and exercise to make sure your body is up to par and in the best state as possible. Your first step may be to grab that pen and paper and begin to write that book, begin to write that song, or sign up for a club at school. Whatever your first step might be, take it. Begin to create short term and long term goals. When putting the work in and grinding for your dreams, you must have discipline and approach every day as if it were your last. You must discipline and hold yourself accountable at all times by sticking to those short term and long term goals. Set expectations for yourself every single day. Set time aside each day to operate in your passion by making a daily list of things to do. Every day you're not going to want to work as hard, and that's understandable. Be mindful to not lose too much time because time is of the essence, and you must treat it as such. Remember that we get what we focus on, so focus on what you want out of life because everything is not a priority. Begin doing what you love to do today and without regret. Become great today because you've been called to be great by putting your time and talents into action every day. While achieving those goals and dreams, remember those deadlines, take your time, and go day by day. Don't allow fear and hesitation to keep you from the

BEST SEASON OF YOUR LIFE. You have the tools, courage, faith, and knowledge to turn your dreams into a reality!

# *Dear Son, I Promise!*

*To my only son, my miracle baby, Aiden Tre'Veon* Harris: I remember the day your mother called me and told me you would be here in nine months. I was working at Dominos in Raeford, North Carolina. The phone call made my heart skip a beat and literally land on the pizza cutting table. You've changed my life and have made me the man I am today. You're so wise at such a young age. I'm so proud of the man I know you will be. It's an honor to call you, son. I'm raising you to embrace quality and to live and have the best life possible. I'm honored to cover you, and I'm excited to see what you do with the talents and gifts God has given you. I am confident that you will turn them into an inheritance and take the family's name to the next dimension! If I can only be half the father that you are the son, I'd be the best dad in the entire world. I love you, Aiden!

# About the Author

*Quentin T. Harris has been performing on stage and in* a bevy of productions for over fifteen years. Throughout his career, he has been in numerous television and entertainment ventures. Some of his work has also been released on various networks; such as the Oprah Winfrey Network (OWN), B.E.T., MTV, TV One and LifeTime. Quentin has worked with several producers and writers, including Tyler Perry and Steve Harvey. He has even hosted some of the most elite events in the Metro Atlanta area.

It was Quentin's passion for entertainment that sparked an interest in his recent move to Atlanta, GA. The unstoppable performer is currently working on three different stage plays, two television shows that will release on major networks this year, a new web talk show based on all of the hottest social media outlets and his very own Radio Show, "Q in the Streets," and he is scheduled to tour intentionally. The show, featured on WTNT 107.7 features Quentin and two other co-hosts, with a mission to ignite a thought-provoking and engaging platform that supports and encourages audiences to share their views and use their gifts to turn their dreams into reality because dreams are real.

Quentin's experiences allow him to travel extensively, attending some of the "most talked about" elite events on the east and west coasts. Despite his busy schedule, as a CEO/Founder, he still finds time for his non-profit organization, “DreamsAreReal.” After the release of his highly anticipated book "Dreams Are Real," Mr. Harris has now directed his focus towards a plethora of projects that allow him to keep his hands in motion in the entertainment business. Quentin Harris is also a father to a gifted seven-year-old son named Aiden Harris! As he always says #DreamsAreReal!

# *Connect with Quentin Harris on Social Media*


Quentin Tre'Veon Harris

C.E.O - QTH Enterprise LLC
Author
Actor
TV Personality
Radio Personality- #QInTheStreets

Instagram: @QuentinHarris21

http://quentinharrisenterprises.bigcartel.com/

(404) 946-3196

www.ingramcontent.com/pod-product-compliance
Ingram Content Group UK Ltd.
Pitfield, Milton Keynes, MK11 3LW, UK
UKHW020136250726
13967UKWH00002B/691